POETIC MEDITATIONS

By John E. DeCock

Order this book online at www.trafford.com
or email orders@trafford.com

Most Trafford titles are also available at major online book retailers.

Printed in the United States of America.

ISBN: 978-1-4269-7489-2 (sc)
ISBN: 978-1-4269-7490-8 (hc)
ISBN: 978-1-4269-7491-5 (e)

Library of Congress Control Number: 2011911211

Trafford rev. 08/30/2011

 www.trafford.com

North America & international
toll-free: 1 888 232 4444 (USA & Canada)
phone: 250 383 6864 ♦ fax: 812 355 4082

THE POET:

Who is John E. DeCock?

Missionary John, a distant relative of the late Corrie Ten Boom (author of "The Hiding Place"), was born and raised in the Netherlands, where he met Thelma, who later became his wife and spiritual partner.

From his early youth, John believed that he would become a missionary. Home, church, and especially Sunday school, had a great influence in forming this life vision. He loved missionary stories, especially since the pastor and his wife of the little church the family attended, had been missionaries in Venezuela.

Once John and Thelma were engaged, they prayed for direction for their lives, and felt strongly that they should immigrate to the United States. In 1961, they married in North Highland, CA, in February, 1962.

Their honeymoon was their first journey to the mission field, in Surinam, South America. There they were involved in church pioneering in the city of Paramaribo. After a year and two months, they went back to the States to further their college education.

In 1966, their first son, (Andrew) Marc, was born, and in 1967 they returned to Surinam to continue their mission work.

In 1973, during a furlough in the US, they were blessed with another son, Michael (Mike) Phillip.

In 1976 they returned once more to the States. While there, they were led to make a change of their mission field. A new door opened in the northern part of Belgium, in Flanders. Again, they were involved in church pioneering. Thelma started a ministry among women, called "Women's Aglow." John was involved in a radio ministry and helped in a fellowship of churches which were encouraging different outreaches in the area.

In 1999, another door opened. This time it was on a small southern Caribbean island, called Bonaire. Again, it was pasturing and helping to build a church building.

They finally retired in 2003. John's physical problems became a hindrance to further travel. They greatly miss the work and all the

Nationals with whom they had been so close, but they feel they are still missionaries at heart.

Although John had done some poetry as sermon illustrations, and in correspondence, he feels that at this time in his life it might be right to put some of the things , about which he had been preaching, into poetry form.

E-mails are one of the ways he is using to stay in touch with friends around the world.

His poems are often forwarded and are also being printed in church bulletins. They are available to ministers for use in their sermons.

John is still involved in teaching and is leading a very lively and spiritually active bible study for seniors.

THE DEDICATION:

I would like to dedicate this little bundle of poems to Thelma, my lovely wife of almost 50 years. We have worked together in so many places; she has often given me her wise advice, and as partner, mother of our two sons, and grandmother of our two grandsons, she filled the place God has given her beside me with patience and much love.

I LOVE YOU, HONEY!

John

PREFACE:

Fans of Christian poetry are in for a wonderful experience when they read the poems of John DeCock. John has been writing poetry for many years and has finally decided to publish his favorites. As a friend and colleague, I have been blessed by my association with him, in church, in bible studies, and personally.

John was born in Holland and has ministered for the Lord all in different countries. His goal though life has been like that of Saint Paul, someone who has led souls to accept Jesus as their Lord. In publishing this book, John hopes to be able to continue his ministry of leading others to a belief in His Lord and Savior, Jesus Christ. Sit down and relax, turn your eyes on Jesus, and enjoy a generous helping of glorious poetical genius.

Lorna Moreno

Rev. John DeCock and his family have been personal friends and also Ministerial Colleagues of ours for the past 50 years. He is a real Man of God, who spent most of his ministry on the Mission Field, telling people the Good News of the Gospel of Jesus Christ. We appreciate his sincere love and dedication for the Lord.

He is very talented and has written many poems. They come from his life experiences and straight from his heart. Many people have been touched and inspired by these poems, including ourselves.

We know you will enjoy this book, and our prayer is that you will be ministered to and encouraged by these writings.

In Christ's Service,
Rev. Larry & Ellawena Tuton

TABLE OF CONTENTS

A THIEF IN THE NIGHT

by John E. DeCock

The night is dark, no moon or star,
there's just a quiet breeze.
The roads are empty, there's no car
and no, there's no police.
Except one man who roams around,
from house to house he goes.
Almost invisible, without a sound,
just there, and no one knows.
     Except this creep
     all are asleep,
and dream their time away.
     Behind the door
     you hear them snore,
getting ready for next day.

The man outside, continues on,
from door to door he goes.
He feels around, from dusk to dawn;
"The windows, did men close?"
He checks a door if locked inside,
an entrance to the house.
An open door, he comes in quiet,
yes, quiet as a mouse.
     And then the man
     secures a plan,
to have a quick escape.
     To quickly go,
     you never know
if someone is awake.

He looks around, for treasures small,
diamonds or rings or gold.
The credit cards, he takes them all -
he's quick, but self-controlled.
And then he's gone without a trace,
in darkness of the night.
He wears a smile upon his face
and soon is out of sight.
  He came so fast
   and nothing last
from treasures saved through years.
  This was his trick,
   he went so quick
and left behind great fears.

Nobody saw, nobody heard
and no one did prepare.
At dusk a family got a stirred,
'tall happened unaware.
But as a thief, in mid of night
our Lord will soon appear.
He'll take what's precious in his sight,
the rest he leaves right here.
  Then he goes back
   and in a sec;
the twinkling of an eye,
   he's gone away
   without delay.
Aware the day is nigh.

The question is: "Will you prepare,
get ready for that day?"
"Are you asleep - or well aware,
will you be gone ... or stay?"
"Are you like gold, that's purified?
Or like a precious stone?"
"Like costly jewels within his sight
or like a worthless bone?"
  Now is the hour,
   that by His power
His work be done in you.
   If you permit
    to make you fit, ...
prepare you through and through.

—————————

In Bible time parables taken from the daily world were often used to illustrate spiritual things. If the authors would have lived in our time, they probably would have used the things we daily use as a parable.

Their messages were often put in poetic form. These two considerations gave me the idea to write:

DANGEROUS VIRUS
by John E. DeCock

There is an urgent warning – that some people share;
Have you heard of a virus - that's causing a scare?
Even though your protection -
>   you think is updated,
Beware what your down-loads - and net-search created!
Look out you don't crash! - For identity theft!
Or losing your files - so nothing is left!
Out of your e-mail - a forward is found
Delete will not work –
>   so it's getting around.
Once in your computer – it finds every friend
Forwarding itself -
>   through e-mails you send.
To many computers- it caused major harm,
Heed to the warning - why they sound the alarm.
Ending this problem –
>   so hard to do,
Secure all your files – important to you.
All of your back-ups - are safe and secure;
Virus protected - from this dangerous lure.
If you think now: - "Well let me reboot,
Overriding this danger"- you find that you couldn't.
Utter frustration - may show on your face,
Regarding the files -
>   the virus did erase.

Though this might be awful, - when you lose control,
Have you heard of a virus - which endangers your soul!
Effecting your mind -
                          thoughts you can't delete,
Like with virus infected, - affecting each deed.
Overriding your morals; - and pushing its way,
Releasing its poison, - by night and by day.
Dangers for sure, -
                          now let me explain:
Just like a computer – there are things that remain.
Every memory - has input you see;
Sounds, words and visions, - whatever may be.
Use virus protection - protecting your brain.
Select what you watch -
                          and what you retain.
Come then to the Lord, - a decision you make,
Have you considered: - "Your soul is at stake?"
Remember from all - you heard and have seen,
It's He that can cleanse you, - and the way to be clean,
See the acrostic - and then be advised …
T ……………………………………

_____

HAPPY EVER AFTER
by John E. DeCock

It started when they fell in love,
      like Romeo and Juliet.
Her beauty, charm and personality
was something that you seldom see.
      'Twas love, the moment that they met ...
He knew she was the one, his dove.

'Twas also love from her that day.
      He was so handsome and so strong,
yet tender and compassionate too.
She loved the things that he could do.
      Deep in her heart was a new song.
With him, she really felt okay.

      They'd so much joy and laughter,
      hoping for - happy ever after -

Then came the day that he proposed;
      'Twas romance in extreme.
He met her parents, asked for her hand,
and later to his home they went.
      The happiest pair you've ever seen.
So all went well, and they did toast.

Soon they prepared the wedding day,
      she choose her dress and veil,
prepared the guest list with great care,
they both agreed who should be there,
      put invitations in the mail,
prepared the home where they would stay.

      It caused them joy and laughter,
      planning for - happy ever after -.

W hen all the wedding guests were seated,
        Jesus was there and Mary too,
twelve disciples also there.
They made their vows and said their prayer.
        Their party planned like most would do;
the food and drinks, just what they needed.

Music was great for fun and dancing,
        some speeches, jokes and great advice.
smiles and contentment on the faces.
all things in harmony and good graces,
        the presents practical and nice,
and all décor was so enhancing.

        A day of joy and laughter;
        prepared for - happy ever after -.

But then, it was a great surprise,
        their wine ran out, now what to do?
And water was the only drink.
It made the servers quickly think …
        "Was there an answer? What and who, …
in this dilemma give advice?"

I do not know how Mary heard,
        but soon she told her son,
"They're without wine or other drink:
can you help them, what do you think?
        I'm sure that something can be done,
just help them out and give your word."

        Almost an end to joy and laughter …
        a token for – no happy ever after? -

And then she gave this great advice,
        wherever marriage is in decline,
"Do all what He would ever say!"
And when you do, do not delay.
        For He turns water into wine,
restoring love to your surprise.

Three lessons which this story shows;
        In your own marriage make Him part.
Mary's advice should then be heard
so listen to His precious word."
        He gives you both a brand new start.
Of water and of wine He knows.

        Renewing of all the joy and laughter.
        So, live your - happy ever after -.

IT'S HAPPENING IN OUR TIME

by John E. DeCock

Above the sound of nine eleven
  While manmade structures fail,
Towers come tumbling to the ground
  Security doesn't prevail.
There is a voice ten virgins hear
While waiting for the groom,
"Get up! It's time! The bridegroom comes!
  This darkness leads to doom.
Now fix your lamps and trim the wicks,
  Take care the door will close,
Be wise, oh virgins, do not sleep
  Get wrinkles from your clothes."

Above the roaring hurricane
  As New Orleans is hid,
While people seek for solid ground;
  No place to sleep or sit,
There is a voice God's people hear:
  "Make straight your path, prepare,
Let hills come down, the valleys filled,
  The King comes, be aware!"
"Now listen to the trumpet sounds,
  Heralds prepare the way,
The King is coming on the clouds,
  … no longer will delay".

How violently the earth now quakes;
    Haiti, Chile and Japan,
In Indonesia, China, too
    Tsunamis follow them.
A nuclear power plant's destroyed,
    Radiation fills the air,
Places once safe now full of threats,
    And people flee from there.
These are the signs the wedding of the Lamb
    Is drawing near, at hand.
The bride, the church in spotless white
    … prepared for this great end.

Afghanistan, Iraq in war;
    Hear sounds of bombs and battle.
Korea and Iran are threats,
    And boiling like a kettle.
In all the Middle East uproar,
    And Israel in the center,
"Will she be pushed into the sea?"
    and those that do befriend her?
And in the middle of the night,
    When no one is aware,
Like thieves who come to rob the place,
    The Lord will take his share.

We hear of water shortage, too,
      Of hunger and disease,
Of crops that fail, of floods and droughts,
      While human needs increase.
Will earth be soon in Satan's rule?
      … the beast and antichrist?
Oh, faithful … be the best you can
      And no, be not surprised.
For in the twinkling of an eye,
      Christ will return at last.
We'll all be changed, taken away,
      Your King will manifest.

There comes a voice from oil rich lands:
      "Islam will take the earth."
The stocks at once are tumbling down,
      Our homes have lost their worth.
Foreclosures over all the land,
      Retirement funds decay,
Employment seized for working class,
      Security did not stay.
"When all these signs have come to pass,
      Oh, Church, lift up your head,
Salvation now is drawing near!"
      It's what the Master said.

When Jesus started His ministry He called the twelve disciples to follow and learn from Him. Philip was one of them. It didn't take much time for Philip to become a witness. I suppose that at that time his knowledge of Jesus and His ministry was limited. But the least he could say, to someone who was full of questions, was, "Come and see!" And there we have the story of ...

NATHANAEL
by John E. DeCock

There is a mention of a man,
whose story should be told.
And let me try as well I can
his secret to unfold.

He was an Israelite, indeed,
who walked in righteousness.
He did not lie, he did not cheat
and stood for faithfulness.

Nathanael which means: "Gift from God",
A precious lovely name.
Bartholomew some scholars thought,
is probably just the same.

His character was shaped by law.
In synagogue and schools.
Examples in his home he saw;
God formed him with these tools.

There's little written in the Word,
except what Jesus said,
when Philip brought him to the Lord,
the first time that they met.

We do not know what did transpire
one day under a tree,
but Jesus knew his heart's desire,
his longing He did see.

He was a man without deceit,
still he felt emptiness
and looking for the truth indeed
he searched without success.

Until that day when Philip came,
And this is what he said:
"We found the Christ and you should come,
He lives in Nazareth."

Nathanael did truly fear;
"Could good come from that place?"
No scripture did he ever hear;
that town had no such grace.

Nathanael was an honest man.
He walked on solid ground.
And only followed faithful then
what in God's Word is found.

And Jesus saw his honesty;
The time he spent in prayer.
His longing underneath his tree,
He knew what happened there.

"You are the One we're looking for!"
Nathanael did exclaim.
He knew he had to search no more
and so with Christ remained.

Among the twelve that Jesus chose
Bartholomew had his place.
Three years they walked and were so close
and talked from face to face.

From that day on, I'm not surprised,
he always did proclaim
the Gospel of the living Christ,
did wonders in his Name.

He spread the message without fear.
Many were saved and blessed.
And being fruitful year to year,
he gave his life at last.

Please see the lesson if you can,
'tis "When you seek you'll find,
and for the honesty in men,
the Lord is never blind."

————————————

ONESIMUS
by John E. DeCock

A wonderful story I would like to tell,
so often forgotten, but we would do well,
to remember what happened to a slave one day,
who liked to be free and did run away.
  Before he proceeded,
   he stole what he needed.
Then journeyed to Rome, the world of his dreams,
to celebrate freedom in this land of extremes.

This mention I should make; a runaway slave
is the worst you can be, regardless how brave.
In old Roman culture, I don't know if you have heard,
they're least of society, I give you my word.
  Yes, all will reject them
   and no one protect them.
Even worse than the life of a slave, understand,
is the life of a runaway slave in the end!

And so Onesimus (for that is his name),
made that long journey, till to Rome he came.
And there he met Paul and his fortune would be,
who told him of Christ, who really sets free!
  And deep in his soul
   the Lord took control.
There was peace; there was joy and new life begun,
the happiest life found under the sun.

But there was a problem, what's right than is right!
He still was a slave from his master in flight.
So Paul wrote a letter to Philemon, you see,
requesting his owner to set the man free.
   He offered to pay
    the debts of this stray.
So the slave with the letter for the final solution
went home to his master to make restitution.

This would be the end of the story, my friend,
the letter is still in the Bible as sent.
But soon there's a letter that Ignatius wrote,
who was a great bishop, we will find a quote
   concerning a bishop,
    doing a great job.
A wonderful man and what is his name?
'twas Bishop Onessimus of Smyrna who came.

Of course they could not give a DNA test
if both were the same and God, He knows best.
A bishop who formerly was a runaway slave?
So radically changed through the power Jesus gave?
   For new life was found
    that changed things around!
And I know for sure and often have seen
the change God can make, is to the extreme!

In all of our lives we have times of disappointment. Things do not always go the way we have expected them to go; even the things we thought were deeply rooted in our faith.

This was the experience of the two men on their way to Emmaus. But many things that they suffered were because they had misunderstood the scriptures and they had not paid close attention to all that Jesus said. It is so easy to believe in the things we like, and leave out the things we don't. But, let us go on and I hope you will find encouragement in the next story...

ON THE WAY TO EMMAUS
by John E. DeCock

How sadly they walked,
how despondently talked,
their feet were as heavy as lead.
Their hope was all spent,
to Emmaus they went,
their hearts being full of regret.
They'd looked for a day
when without delay
the enemy would be defeated.
All Roman oppression
would end without question;
an end to the way they were treated.

But nothing went right
when they crucified
their Lord, He, the source of their hope.
So clouded their mind
their mood did so blind
that they were not able to cope.
And neither aware
who walked with them there,
He showed them what scripture foretold;
'twas all in God's plan
again and again,
predicted with promise so bold.

As a lamb He was slain.
For believers great gain;
full forgiveness from sin was so bought.
Our debts did He pay
and on the third day
He arose to the glory of God.
And while they were walking
they kept up their talking.
They finally arrived at their door.
The light growing dim
they welcomed Him in;
They longed for such news even more.

They sat at his feet
and soon they did eat
and they saw, when He took up the bread;
The scars in his hand
made them understand
He has risen, 'twas just as He said.
They wasted no time,
turned around on a dime.
"Our Savior is risen indeed."
Proclaiming the news
among Gentiles and Jews,
the hope for a people in need.

Oh, glory divine,
this Savior is mine.
He conquered both death and the grave.
Even when I don't see
He is walking with me,
and walking with him, I am safe.
Sometimes through all care,
wondering: "Is He still there?"
But He said He would never forsake.
With wine and bread broken
a message unspoken;
his presence … when we do partake.

PETER'S DARKEST NIGHT
by John E. DeCock

How could I ever have denied,
my Savior, Lord and Friend,
the day He suffered and He died?
I cannot understand.

Once I confessed to Him my faith:
"The Christ, God's Son are you!"
I knew He saves us by his grace,
God's promises come true.

I said: "My Lord I'll stay with you.
No, I will never leave,
whatever other men may do,
Lord, I'll bear any grief."

But that dark night, they captured Him
and scorned Him in their hate,
I stood there in the light so dim
close by the fire they'd made.

"Are you not one of them?" they cried:
"You are from Galilee!"
" 'Twas you who drew his sword to fight
there in Gethsemane!"

Three times I said, three times I lied:
"That man, I know Him not!"
It is my Lord, whom I denied,
the only Son of God.

The rooster crowed that early morn'.
He turned and looked my way.
My words had caused Him deeper scorn
than all they did and say.

Yes, after all He's done and taught,
his love in every way,
I tell a girl, "I know Him not",
My Lord I did betray.

I fled the scene into the night.
in deep despair and shame;
how could I ever make this right,
how could I clear my name?

No deeper pain I ever found,
the agony of soul …
It felt like hell was all around.
I cried beyond control.

They mocked and tried Him and they lied,
with thorns they crowned His head.
'Twas by the fire that I denied:
"I know Him not!" I said.

That day He gave his life, my Lord;
upon a cross He died …
"How can I ever be restored?"
in agony I cried.

Peter means rock, that is my name,
it means stability.
But I confess, and it's with shame,
'tis weakness that I see.

I always thought that I was strong;
"On me you can rely,"
but in that hour it proved me wrong!
'Tis for His grace I cry.

That day, there was no hope for me,
went fishing once again;
the nets and boat upon the sea.
Our labor was in vain.

But in the early morning light
a fire of coal I see …
I hear his voice across the tide,
He waited there for me.

I failed Him, but He didn't fail.
There on the shore He stood.
I came, aware of my betrayal,
as quickly as I could.

His words were chosen with great care,
He asked, "Do you love me?"
I felt no condemnation there,
He spoke so tenderly.

I answered Him in truth that day,
"Yes, Lord, You see within."
My shame I could not hide away;
embarrassed for my sin.

That day He lovingly restored
and took my sins away!
Yes, three times were His loving words,
three times I heard Him say, …

"Protect my lambs and feed my sheep,
I put them in your care."
"I'll go with you and you I'll keep;
protect you everywhere."

And now I shout for joy and peace,
let everybody hear,
"He is alive and He forgives
and takes away our fear."

The joy of Easter is in Him;
He lives restoring men.
He saves and makes us free from sin.
COME TO HIM WHILE YOU CAN!

Jesus often took His parables from the countryside. He spoke about the vineyard, about the seed, a field, and the man who sowed the seed. Paul took his illustrations more from city life: a temple, a building, or the army.

On one occasion he compared the Christian with a soldier who needed to be prepared for battle...

THE BATTLE CRY
by John E. DeCock

Be strong, oh, army of the Lord.
Stand in God's mighty power.
Unite and be in one accord;
get ready for this hour.

Put on full armor, stop your dreams.
Let's take our stand today
against the Devil's dirty schemes;
the fight has come our way.

Our struggle is not with a man
of flesh and blood, you know,
but 'tis with Satan and his clan;
against a spiritual foe.

The rulers and authorities;
the forces of the night,
our combat's high priorities.
Now let's get up - and fight.

Take care that in the evil day,
we all can stand our ground
and in the battle gear we may
be firm and faithful found.

Let's put the truth around us now
and hear the battle cries.
Let's buckle up, get ready now,
defeat deceit and lies.

The breastplate will protect the heart,
guard us with righteousness;
Of hate or envy have no part
of jealousy or bitterness.

With readiness on both our feet,
the Gospel to proclaim,
ready to move and act with speed;
to go in Jesus name.

So let us join our shields of faith.
With darts he will attack.
The foe has come in his mad rage,
but we will push him back.

Put on the helmet of salvation;
protect your thoughts and mind.
Beware of Satan's infiltration;
for his deceit, be deaf and blind.

Then take in hand the Spirit's sword;
be ready to proceed
and fight the battle with God's word,
till demons see defeat.

And pray to God for everything,
as often as you can,
in Spirit, all requests then bring.
He knows our battle plan.

And victory will soon be ours
because of Calvary;
and Satan and his ugly powers
will final judgment see!

When we think of Christmas, we think of a great celebration. And rightly so, for the Son of God joined us here on earth because we were separated from the Father and He being completely out of our reach. But this way the Father reached out to us to bring us back to Himself.

When we think of Easter, we are reminded of the pain and the suffering it cost to unite us with the Father, and the glorious words: "It is finished!" The way to God is open now. We also think of the triumphant resurrection on Easter morning; Death and the grave are defeated.

But how are we celebrating Ascension Day? The glorious day the Lord came home from his journey here on earth and presented his finished work to the Father; the day He was crowned with glory and honor. Come on, let us celebrate Ascension Day.

THE LORD'S ASCENSION
by John E. DeCock

Let's celebrate the Lord's ascension;
>   The day the Father brought Him home
And all of heaven in attention
>   Was gathered round The Great White Throne.
And in the midst the Lamb was standing,
>   His work was finished to the end.
With trumpet sounds of praise ascending
>   to Him who to the earth was sent.
His work was done. The only Son,
>   He paid the price, so men could rise
from chains of sin, and enter in
>   the Holy place, by saving grace.

Let's join in heaven's celebration,
Let's all present our loud ovation.

Now listen to the Father's voice.
>   Like thunder rolls our God is speaking,
"All men on earth will have a choice
>   from the most powerful to the weakling."
So all may come and bow their knee,
>   confess Him as their Lord and Savior.
And then through Him be truly free
>   from bondage to his bad behavior.
"My Son obeyed, was not afraid,
>   went down to hell, now all is well,
The prison open, dominion broken.
>   The prisoner's free, Satan did flee."

Let's join in heaven's celebration,
Let's all present our loud ovation.

Now hear the Father's glorious word,
        "Come up, my Son, to my right hand.
Here is your throne, let it be heard
        I lift your Name in every land.
In heaven and on earth be known,
        there is no higher greater power.
Above all kings and every throne
        from this day on, this very hour.
And yes, indeed, under your feet
        your very soul Satan's control.
A glorious bride, be on your right.
        Sure I take care, she will prepare."

Let's join in heaven's celebration.
Let's all present our loud ovation.

It is not wise to compare the road you have to walk with that of others. They are all different. You will not be able to carry your neighbor's burdens, but the strength you have received will be sufficient for your need. With this truth in mind, I wrote my next poem.

THE WAY GOD LEADS

by John E. DeCock

The way God will lead is different each time;
some roads go through sunshine and joy,
sometimes they are rugged, steep mountains to climb,
sometimes we feel tossed like a toy.
       Whatever it'll be,
       be sure He will see,
his hand will protect and sustain.
       His arm is so strong,
       He'll lead us along,
His love will forever remain.

Sometimes the wild storm will be stilled at his word;
He calls with strong voice, "Peace, be still!"
The waves will be calm when His voice will be heard,
they're subject at once to His will.
       But sometimes the boat
       will not stay afloat;
like Paul who was shipwrecked one day.
       For God had a plan
       that was different then,
He saved many people that way.

For Peter, one time, the doors of the jail
were opened as an answer to prayer.
The chains were all broken at believers prevail
and soon in their midst he stood there.
       But not every jail
       let go without bail,
for John behind bars did remain.
       But there God revealed
       His plan that was sealed
and the message was never the same.

God's people, once slaves, later traveled around
and after they lived in the land
their rulers were Judges, then a kingdom was found
until far away they were sent.
> After Babylon you see
> they never were free
even though they returned to their land.
> For from that same hour
> under foreign power
with oppression they had to contend.

But through all affliction, in fullness of time
God sent His own Son among men,
to pay for the sins of yours and of mine,
it all happened according to plan.
> So do understand
> in things God has planned
all circumstances do have their place.
> He still has control
> fulfilling His goal,
the victory is God's in the end.

Remember my friend, just trust in God's word,
there's no pain or no suffering in vain.
Hold on to God's hand, the promise you've heard,
for His promise is: "He will sustain."
> Now stop to compare
> with others out there,
your life and your way are unique.
> But rest in God's grace
> and walk just by faith,
be sensitive when God will speak.

THE WISE MEN
Poem by John E. DeCock

They came from the east and they followed a star.
        There was a shortness of light.
Their journey so long for they came from afar
        The Christ-child was born in the night.
Now who were these Magi? What caused them to go?
        'Tis a riddle and I have no clue.
There are fables and stories, some think that they know,
        But is what they think really true?
But whatever they say, - around Christmas day
        I'm sure you heard it before.
The questions remain - "How come that they came
        To the Christ-child so they could adore?"

Don't think that the riddle will be answered by me
        Regardless how fast I may write.
For I take the story from Mathew you see
        No new revelation or light.
But there must be a reason why God's word included,
        Why forever this story is told,
And just in this season it is deeply rooted
        Within our tradition so bold.
The lessons I found - will turn this around,
        So don't throw this poem away.
A devotional thought - that's just what I got.
        I hope it will help on your way

These Magi or wise men, astronomers, kings
        Had only the light of the star.
And this was their wisdom among other things
        They came even though it was far.
Their journey was long, but they followed the light
        Regardless how rugged the way.

They pressed to their goal by day and by night
     No thing or no men made them stray.
And that I call wisdom; it led them to freedom
     Even though their knowledge was small,
With searching and asking - and earnestly seeking
     They did find the King, after all.

And when they had found Him they worshipped, 'tis told,
     Their treasures they laid at His feet.
Their incense and myrrh and valuable gold.
     Great sacrifice from them, indeed.
'Twas myrrh for His death, 'twas gold for their King
     And incense for He was their God.
Together with treasures their hearts they did bring
     To Him they surrendered their lot.
And after they stayed - and after they prayed
     No longer the star led the way.
By God they were led - by a dream it is said.
     They'd learned God's voice to obey.

 Now set up your camels, your kings, and your star,
     And all of the nice decoration,
Sing old songs of Magi that came from afar
     And came with such great adoration.
Get ready for Christmas with gifts and with food,
     Invite all your kin to a meal.
With songs of the season get in the right mood
     With ham or with turkey or veal.
But whatever you do - know one thing is true
     These Magi were wise men, indeed.
I hope you will see - what Christmas should be
     And that you will follow their lead.

THE WORD BECAME FLESH
By John E. DeCock

He is the Word of God and God himself in essence.
All things by Him were made, in the Creator's presence.
     Not that I understand,
     Able to comprehend
     But He came down to men
     According to God's plan.
And they beheld the Son's own glory.
It is recorded as the Gospel story.

He is the prophetic Word, through many prophets given
In fullness of the time, fulfilled among the living.
     The Father, we are told,
     Men did in Him behold.
     And Jesus was his name,
     The Son of God who came.
He will return to earth, we heard,
According to prophetic Word.

He is the Word of power, God spoke and all was made.
Stars, sun, moon and the earth, by Words God did create.
     When to this world He came
     His power was the same;
     The storm and wind and sea
     Obeyed at once - you see.
And when He spoke, - his word was sent
Things really changed, at his command.

He is the Word of truth, revealing all deception.
The way, the truth, the life, yes, truth without exception.
     Within a world of lies
     He came and paid the price
     To set his people free
     From all impurity.
Thus righteousness He brought
In words and deeds and thought.

He is the Word of wisdom, revealed at early age;
The Scribes and Pharisees, they marveled at such grace.
> Later they tried to trick
> With schemes that would not stick.
> But simple men who heard
> Found guidance in His word.
Still men today of every race
Find words of wisdom by His grace.

He is the Word of knowledge, the Word of revelation
To teach us heavenly truths as part of our salvation.
> Even a child can know
> And so in knowledge grow
> Things hidden for the wise
> Incomprehensible in size
But still revealed unto the meek
When they with all their heart will seek.

He is the Spirit's Word, often revealed through tongues,
A language made in heaven, inspiring Spiritual songs.
> When we are Spirit filled,
> Our sinful flesh is killed,
> The Spirit helps our prayer
> And we become aware
That God will take the helm's control,
The Word the compass of our soul.

———————————————

The day of Pentecost is another important celebration for the church. For the Jew, it was the celebration of the giving of the Law and also it became a harvest festival. For the Christian church, Pentecost is the celebration of the giving of the Holy Spirit and the birth of the Church. I hope it will be for you a special day filled with God's Spirit, and a day of rejoicing that you are a part of that church. God Bless you!

THIS IS IT
by John E. DeCock

From north and south, from east and west
        they'd come, the elderly and young,
to celebrate the yearly feast
        with music, dancing and with song.
Rejoicing for law once given,
        they celebrated harvest time.
With great devotion they were driven,
        with praise and thanks to the Devine.

Then something happened in Jerusalem.
        A new phenomenon took place.
For somewhere in an upper chamber,
        some Christians acted in strange ways.
They heard a wind, than they saw fire
        and all the Christians spoke in tongues.
They acted drunken of the Spirit
        and people gathered in great throngs.

Now what was this? What did transpire?
It was the Holy Ghost with fire!

This is what Joel once predicted.
        For from his prophesy we know
That in the latter days the Spirit
        will fall on men and gifts bestow.
Your sons that day will then have visions
        and dreams He gives to older men.
Prophetic utterance, revelations,
        for latter days, this is God's plan.

This is what John, the Baptist spoke of
        when he saw Christ near Jordan's shore.
He said: "I baptize you in water
        but He is worthy so much more.
With Holy Ghost and fire He'll baptize.
        He is the Lamb of God who came.

Prepare the way make straight the highway.
        There is Salvation in his Name."

Now this was it what did transpire.
It was the Holy Ghost and fire!

This is what the Lord Jesus spoke of.
        He prophesied, "I'll go away.
But I'll leave you not as the orphans,
        the Spirit comes and He will stay."
He is the comforter from the Father,
        the Holy Spirit from above.
He'll guide and teach and give you power,
        stay in Jerusalem, stay in love!

Then Peter spoke, "This all is written,
        they are not drunk or filled with wine.
It's only nine AM and early,
        this promise is all yours and mine."
"What must we do?" the people asked him.
        "What must we do this very hour?"
"Repent, be baptized," Peter answered
        "and Christ will baptize you with power."

Now this is it what will then transpire.
He'll send the Holy Ghost with fire!

With prophesies, with dreams and visions,
        the Holy Spirit will descend.
Upon the parents and the children
        from that day forth until the end.
Upon the rulers and the servants,
        upon all men both great or small.
Until God's Spirit fills the planet,
        His knowledge spreads to one and all!

There are stories in the Bible that make your hair stand up straight. But it teaches us that even the great men of Bible times had their failures. Sounds familiar? These stories, however, are in the Bible so we could learn from them and not just point a nasty finger. Well, let me pull out of an almost forgotten corner, the name of:

URIAH
by John E. DeCock

There was a brave, great solder,
Uriah was his name.
He fought for God, for Israel and her king.
Willing to sacrifice most anything.
    But on the battlefield he needed
        his backup just the same.
-Oh king, back up ... Uriah!-

Then there was the great king, David.
        who skipped this time the war.
He stayed at home and followed the reports,
commanded moves with his cohorts.
    In selfishness he'd got his way;
        sin lingered at the door.
-While on the front ... Uriah.-

There was this gorgeous beauty.
        Bathsheba was her name.
She bathed and David looked with lustful eyes
He wanted her at any price.
    He sent for her and took her in.
        He acted without shame.
-The sweetheart of ... Uriah.-

Now he had got her pregnant,
        Uriah was at war.
And David tried to cover up his deed
"Come home Uriah for I need
    to talk with you, then go back home
        and love your wife once more."
-This way he needs ... Uriah?-

The king's plan didn't work that day.
    Uriah's solidarity
kept him from going home; the army was at war.
His character we sure adore.
    So David could not save his royal name;
      his pretense of morality.
-His problem was … Uriah.-

One lustful sin needed cover up,
    a second at his door.
'Twas treason which now filled his mind,
"Withdraw backup of any kind!"
    David became the enemy of his friend
      who trusted him before.
-And so they killed … Uriah.-

The widow was Bathsheba.
    She married him in the end.
But God wouldn't let him get away with it;
two sins, God, in the law, forbid.
    His punishment was on the way,
      but David did repent.
-Now what about … Uriah.-

The Davids of our time are leaders,
    Bathsheba their desire,
Uriah stands for those who pay the price
For treason, which is never nice;
    Withdrawing needed backing up
      to them who face the fire.
-The sin against … Uriah.-

'Tis lust and greed and also pride
    that caused abuse of power.
Good people often deeply hurt you know.
If you caused pain, don't just let go!
    Help heal the wounds that you have caused!
      Do what you can this hour!
-Do you have a … Uriah?-

WHAT 'S IN YOUR HAND
by John E. DeCock

When God calls men, He's able to,
Regardless of what men can do.
>   And men might say, "Oh Lord, I can't,"
>   His answer is: -"What's in your hand?"-

Although He once made nature's laws,
Also can break them for His cause.
>   For He is God and has the power
>   Above all else this very hour.

Moses was ordered' "You must go
To Egypt's court and tell Pharaoh,
>   Tell him to let my people free,
>   Free them so they can worship Me."

But Moses said' "Lord, I can't speak;
Stand up to Pharaoh? I'm too weak!"
>   The answer was, "Who made your mouth?
>   I can give words in Pharaoh's house."

And furthermore -"What's in your hand? -
Give it to Me, I made you stand
>   For Pharaoh's court, magicians too
>   And what I want, I make them do!"

So Moses had a shepherd's rod
'Twas from that day the rod of God
>   And now what Moses could not do
>   He did with God and with those two ...

There was no limit to the power
A principle for every hour.
>   This is when men by God is sent
>   And on God's power he will depend.

One day there was a major fight,
A giant had appeared in sight.
        And David, just a shepherd boy
        Compared to him just like a toy.

They tried the armor of the king
But he was better with his sling.
        And trusting God, he took his stand.
        For God once said, -"What's in your hand?"-

For God and boy and sling you see
Are still a large majority.
        The giant bit the dust that day
        And victory was on the way.

One day there was a desperate need;
Five thousand men, nothing to eat
        Except one boy who brought a lunch
        Ready to eat a real nice munch.

But just before to lunch he went
He thought of - what was in his hand. -
        He laid it all at Jesus feet
        And for that hour was no more need.

Now this one thing, and it is true,
It is not just what you can do.
        For whosoever God will send
        He works through - what is in His hand. -

———————-

WORSHIP
by John E. DeCock

When coming to the throne of God in prayer and adoration
I bring the incense of my praise, the joy of my Salvation.
       And then I seek His Holy face
       In worship and in reverent praise;
When coming to the throne of God.

When worship flows from deep within I sense his holiness.
Before Him I become aware of my own sinfulness.
       My conscience now awakes in me
       That what I truly am I see;
When worship flows from deep within.

Coming in Spirit and in truth He cleanses me deep within
And by His blood He washes me and makes me free from sin.
       Now I am pure from head to sole
       For by his grace I am made whole;
Coming in spirit and in truth.

Quietly abiding close to Him, He gives me revelation.
God's truth will totally fill my mind, I bow in admiration.
       No longer am I spiritually blind,
       Eternal worth now fills my mind;
Quietly abiding close to Him.

In fellowship with the Devine, I feel His love's embrace.
Here all life's pains will fade away, in overwhelming grace.
       Now close to Him I long to stay.
       He is more precious every day;
In fellowship with the Devine.

His beauty touches me within and His creating power
Stirs creativity in me, more precious every hour.
        Again His image in me wakes
        Pure new imagination quakes;
His beauty touches me within.

He also shows his ways to me, a goal for all I am.
There is no greater purpose than his everlasting plan.
        I now surrender my own will,
        His plan is better, greater still;
It's all I really want to be.

—————————-

There is nothing new under the sun. There were always people who cheated their way through life and lived without any compassion or conscience. They are unscrupulous and don't consider the pains they cause. The news is full of characters like these. But in the days that Jesus walked the earth we find some, too. One was called:

ZACCHAEUS
by John E. DeCock

We know he was a little man
      who lived in Jericho.
To quickly save, he had a plan,
      'twas evil, sly and low.

For Romans he collected tax,
      and served himself as well.
His slyness reached the very max;
      his ways came straight from hell.

Now Jericho was rich indeed;
      the Romans were aware.
They sold that job to men with greed
      for fairness they'd no care.

Zacchaeus, for this was his name,
      indeed had plenty dough.
But on that day that Jesus came
      he had to hide, you know.

He found a sycamore tree that day;
      it was an ideal plan.
To climb up high so he could stay
      well hidden there from men.

His popularity so low
      in spite of all his loot;
No friends and plenty men his foe
      ready to give the boot.

The Lord stood still under the tree
      He called the little man
"I must go to your home, you see,
      as quickly as I can".

At once the little squirt came down,
  took Jesus home with zest.
Surprising to the rest of town,
  that He would be his guest.

Soon in the villa where he lived
  in private conversation
they talked of God and his great gift,
  the way of true salvation.

Now I don't know what Jesus said,
  but make my own conclusion
from other scriptures which I've read
  and they leave no confusion.

No one can serve two lords, you know,
  our God, and Mammon, too.
Make up your mind who has to go,
  and what you want to do!

Also, the law required pay back
  four times for all he cheated.
Compassion for the poor no lack,
  giving to those who need it.

At once this scrooge had changed his ways;
  became a generous man.
He chose God's will for all his days;
  for all mankind His plan.

When we meet Christ and He comes in,
  we find our life's solution.
He cleanses us, makes free from sin;
  But part is … restitution.
